Octavia:

Guthrie and Beyond

Poetry by Naomi Long Madgett:

Songs to a Phantom Nightingale (1941)
One and the Many (1956)
Star by Star (1965, 1970)
Pink Ladies in the Afternoon (1972, 1990)
Exits and Entrances (1978)
Phantom Nightingale: Juvenilia (1981)
Octavia and Other Poems (1988)
Remembrances of Spring: Collected Early Poems (1993)
Octavia: Guthrie and Beyond (2002)

Octavia:

Guthrie and Beyond

Poems by
Naomi Long Madgett

Detroit
LOTUS PRESS
2002

Grateful acknowledgment is made to Third
World Press for permission to reprint this
portion of *Octavia and Other Poems*. We are
also grateful to Leisia Duskin for her art
opposite the opening poem.

Lotus Press, Inc.
Post Office Box 21607
Detroit, Michigan 48221

In memory of my brothers,
Clarence Marcellus Long, Jr.
and
Wilbur Franklin Long

Contents

Foreword

One year in the 1980s I received an invitation to submit some of my work to a special issue of the literary magazine at the University of Kansas featuring material by contemporary African Americans. It occurred to me that, since my aunt Octavia had been an alumna, it might be appropriate to write a poem about her for submission. I did not intend to write an entire book.

My childhood sense of being her reincarnation had long since been submerged in my consciousness, but having become the family archivist in possession of old family photographs, documents, and letters that my father had brought to Detroit in his late years, I had already done some organization of this material. I went about digging out pictures of Octavia, placing a framed one on my dresser. (I later learned that it was the same photo in her yearbook at the University of Kansas taken in 1909.)

As I studied her photo, my old sense of identification with her returned and deepened, and late one night, after I had spent hours at my computer working on other matters, the opening lines of the prologue imposed themselves upon me. From there the poem just kept growing, recreating what I knew of her life from records and comments I had heard as a child. The short poem I had intended to write was never submitted.

During the course of the writing, I made my first trip to Guthrie, Oklahoma, armed with the four addresses from which old letters had been written and several pictures. I had no idea I would find anyone who knew the family. I just wanted to see if the houses were still there, but mainly I wanted to see and *feel* the city. I rented a car and checked into a motel just down the hill from town.

Without having experienced it for myself, I never could have placed Octavia and her family convincingly in this setting. Nor could I have completed the book. I found two of the houses still standing, one boarded up, a mere shack hardly large enough for five people to sleep—and still find room for a piano. The second one has been reconditioned and modernized like many of the old houses there. During my week's stay, the family living there permitted me to go through it.

On my first full day I found out more than I could have ever imagined or hoped for—several elderly ladies who had been Octavia's high school students (one of whom had also been my grandmother's student in first grade) and records at the Oklahoma Territorial Museum. During the week I also found Faver High School, relocated after an explosion years ago, a copy of the yearbook with Octavia's picture, the unchanged little railroad station, and a great deal of information offered by people I met. I used it all in the poem.

Octavia and Other Poems was published in 1988 by Third World Press and won a Creative Achievement Award given by the College Language Association. The same year, it was adopted as required reading in all Detroit public high schools; a set of the book was purchased for every school.

The following year I returned to Guthrie to read from *Octavia* at the Oklahoma Territorial Museum. One of her former students, ninety years old, was present. The curator had removed the boards from the back door of the old house by the creek, and I was able to go inside—a very emotional experience indeed!

Later a documentary film, *A Poet's Voice* (Vander Films), won a Gold Apple Award for Excellence from the National Educational Media Network. This film combines my comments and reading from *Octavia* with interpretations of the poems by ten visual artists in Detroit. It also contains a cameo appearance by James Earl Jones commenting on the universal appeal of poetry. It also includes a number of photographs that are not in the book.

Since the publication of *Octavia and Other Poems,* I have found additional material concerning my aunt, including diplomas and other documents, along with her high school class picture. In addition, my late husband and I spent a week in New Orleans researching my grandfather. In the archives of the Earl Long (no known relation) Library at the University of New Orleans I found a ledger from discarded Leland University records and a printed program that involved my grandparents. At the Amistad Research Center I found a copy of *Who's Who of the Colored Race*, edited by Frank Lincoln Mather (1915), in which he is listed.

I also spent a week in Lawrence, Kansas where I found Octavia's high school class card, the yearbook of the 1909 graduating class, and the building where the high school she attended was located. (The present building, no longer a school, is built on the original foundation.)

In view of this additional information, I realize that *Octavia* contains some factual errors. However, I decided to leave the poems as originally written. While I am interested in accuracy for my own benefit, I feel that factual details should be subservient to my intention to create here a work of literary art. In reprinting the poem under a new title, I have revised the biographical information at the end of the book and updated birth and death records.

My quest for additional information about my family still consumes me, and I will probably continue searching, on my mother's side of the family as well as my father's, for the rest of my life.

NLM
August 29, 2002

Octavia

Another Landscape

In another landscape
I touch my feet to the roof
of an old house.
I settle in to taste
the red clay earth,
hold gently to the ruined shingles
fragile as memory . . . . . .

Nearby a train chugs
toward Topeka.
The dust it disturbs
filters through an open window.
A boy brushes a fleck of it
from his eye. A cinder
imbeds itself in the rice
on his dinner plate.

After the table is cleared
I follow your footsteps
through oppressive heat
to the little wooden bridge nearby
as fireflies flicker
and gathering darkness drowns
your muffled sighs
in the crystal creek.

In another silence, my tongue savors
untold complaints.
I spread my wings and journey
with metaphors of light and shadow
from this old house, abandoned
by years, to a new habitation
I reinvent with words.

Prologue

i.

When as a child I wore your face, Octavia
(three years returned to earth), and christened
with your name, set forth on my own odyssey,

I had no clothing of my own, only
depressive hand-me-downs, frayed remnants
of someone else's outgrown legacy.

My father dressed me in your skin,
and such a garment, woven of his fabrication
of a second chance, was not to be discarded easily.

ii.
Gagged on emulsions, tonics, and home remedies
contrived to save me from your early death,
I was injected with your blood. Your spirit
hovered above me like a constant cloud
threatening disaster.

Having escaped your first name
(too poignant a reminder of your brother's grief),
I was still branded with the second,
tormented by chastisement for your careless ways.

iii.
We were sixteen, and your girl-round face
stared from my mirror. Your long curl
fell over my shoulder.

The smoldering coals of your eyes
ignited mine.

3

iv.
How your rebellious words
flung from my mouth
must have grieved my father!

Yet his transcendent love
for both of us
always forgave.

How could he not remember
planting the seed that sprouted
into weeds that choked out my identity?

"You outgrew the likeness," he told me,
but by then it was too late.
Reincarnated in my blood,
you were determined not to die.

v.
Your flesh was bonded to my bones,
my feet shod in your stylish
high-buttoned shoes.
Early discontent creased my forehead
with your frown. Your spirit immersed me
and I sank down and down, swirled
in the whirlpool of your eyes
and drowned . . . .

I.
Copper Earth

Genesis

I.
She from 1866 Victoria,
he from 1856 New Orleans—
Cherokee/Black, French/Spanish/Black—
they came together to make a family.

Through Texas, Arkansas, Kansas, Missouri
they moved, pursuing stability,
dignity, honor, and excellence
in service.

In spite of history's chains,
they came.

II.
And you, Octavia,
firstborn in Waco, Texas in 1885,
the choicest plum on your father's tree:

How did you reconcile that oak piano
that dwarfed your family's temporary little homes
with the sun-bloated hours you worked in cotton fields,
thorns pricking your fingers, blood mingling
with your tears (your mother kissing the wound,
sending you back to earn your share
of coins the family needed to pay another bill)?

How measure your father's college education
against your mother's endless battle
with despair?

How did it feel to live in
the wilderness of those days,
wanting to come out,
wanting to be,
wanting to *be ready*
to walk in Jerusalem just like John?

Oklahoma Territory

A wilderness:
A barren place
a place of chalky skies
of autumn wind and furies
red dust blowing
across the open plains
of discontent.

Autumn, 1902
708 South Second Street
Guthrie, Oklahoma Territory

Cottonwood Creek

Cottonwood creek is rising,
it is rising again. The dying sun
burns a hole through the opal sky.
Heavy air smothers the copper earth;
dark furies churn the waters.

There is no time to wait for Mama's return.
Half-dry laundry must be taken down from the line,
piled into a basket and placed on the highest shelf.
Your voice trumpets orders to the others.

Strip the beds! Stack the mattresses and covers
on top of the piano! Gather the shoes
and coats! Load them on top of the bedclothes!
(As an after thought, you add the towel
you have been working on to the pile.)

Collect some changes of clothing.
Be ready to move to higher ground
the minute Mama gets back.
But she must hurry.

In a few days when you return,
Robert will help Marcellus push the piano
onto the L-shaped stoop to dry.
You and Ethel will help Mama
wash down the walls and disinfect the floor.
The things that cannot be redeemed
will have to be discarded.

It will be weeks before the sun's benevolence
dries out the farthest corner of your lives.

Lawrence, Kansas

I.
The basic preparation that normal school would give
was not enough. You yearned for deeper learning,
more for yourself than for the children
you would teach.

Evenings by lamplight in the house on Alabama Street
where board and lodging were provided,
your books were doors of challenge
that would forever open outward now.

Showers of light revived your parched spirit.
The sudden energy of sun electrified your mind.

Autumn, 1905
Lawrence, Kansas

II.
"I'll try to be in Guthrie a few days
early in June," Papa writes.
"I am going to see Octavia graduate
if I must borrow the money to go.
She needs to be commended for her push
and perseverance, and I don't feel
that I can ever do too much for her.

February 15, 1909
Hot Springs, Arkansas

III.
Before you put your cap on, you pause
to smooth an errant strand of hair.
Your baccalaureate gown is opened
to reveal the new white dress,
bow at high collar, that represents
many weeks of sacrifice.

For years, Papa will show your photograph
to friends, boasting of your degree as if
his meager contributions had accomplished it.

June 9, 1909
University of Kansas

Teacher

Hatless, you trudge through alabaster days
    over the railroad tracks
    raised above the level
    of all but the severest floods
to your fifth grade class at Lincoln School,
    raw winds biting your naked fingers,
    dust searing your eyes.

The furnace is slow to heat
and the only light available
comes through the windows.

    Mama's first grade classroom
    on the floor below
    is even colder, but by ten o'clock
    both will be quite comfortable.

The sweet, high voices of children
    cheer you.
The adoration in their eyes
    warms the dismal atmosphere.
You touch your light to their dark lamps.

Winter, 1909-10
Guthrie, Oklahoma

II.

Dear "Son"

Langston High School

Dear Son,
My school was doing well until three weeks ago
when mumps, measles, and chicken pox broke loose.
Many high school pupils have been out,
but I hope for their early return.

A young Mr. Johnson is rooming where I am.
He seems to have much correspondence with Ethel.
Do you know him?

Hot Springs is on a boom for visitors.
The city is fast filling up with strangers.
My duties as principal seldom permit me
to take advantage of the colored bath house.

Hope you will continue to do well.

Your father,
Frank C. Long

Feby. 15, 1909
Hot Springs

Refinement

My dear Marcellus,
I commend you for the stand
you are taking for Christ
and your determination
to enter the ministry.
I am happy to know
that you have been licensed to preach
and are now at Union. You might send me
the catalogue and allow me to read it.

It is further hoped that you will become
a cultured preacher, refined along all lines,
and not the whining, moaning, and whangdoodling
"befo' de war" variety. Let your education
count for something.

I preach myself one in awhile,
and I am always dignified
and try to let my hearers know
that I am somewhat trained and learned.

Strive to go to the front as a scholar,
pulpit orator, and public man at affairs.
You must educate the people
and not get down to their level.
Write soon and keep me informed of your progress.

Papa Long

Feby. 11, 1910
Hot Springs

Mama

Dear Son,
I am up now but not able to work.
I gave up my school two weeks ago.
Most of my salary last month
went to pay someone for teaching in my place,
doctors' bills and medicine.

I'll get the girls to send you a few dollars
to help you. You got the two dollars
that was sent you first of this month.

I am thankful that I have helped prepare you children
so that you are able to help yourselves,
and if I am oblige to stop work for awhile
I shall feel that you all need not suffer.
Octavia and Ethel have done what they could
since I have been sick. I hope I shall soon
get back my strength.

From your devoted mother.

May 25, 1910
708 South Second Street
Guthrie

III.
Red Dust Blowing

Talk

The sky darkens to a magenta
mirror of your rage. Impossible to stay
in this provincial town, neighbors' eyes
gobbling up your Sunday rides with company
unchaperoned in open carriage.

Letters from Elias beckon you.
A school in Washington may have an opening
after Christmas. By then there will be no one
left at home but you and Mama,
she clucking her disapproval,
lecturing you on propriety.
Why linger here in loneliness?
Go where the air of freedom
cleanses away despair.

Late summer, 1910

A Mighty Rocky Road

Dear Son,
I am so concerned about you.
It takes all a person can do
to make it these days.
It's a mighty rocky road
up the path of right
and hard to climb.
It takes the guidance
of the holy spirit to take you through.
Man nor angels can't do it
and friends can't.

Oh, my dear son, I do hope you may soon begin
to learn human nature better
and to understand how people use deception.
The world no longer offers truth,
justice and protection to the right,
the earnest and faithful. All must suffer.

I hope the Lord may make you strong
and that you may go forth in this wicked world
as a light for our people.

Oh, do you know the situation? Do you observe
how the colored race in many cases
is going downward? Just think how some men
are making a living by selling out
and destroying the race.

Your devoted mother

Sept. 30, 1910

Another Autumn

Gray.
Gray wind.
Gray sky.
Gray particles of air
clogging your nostrils,
your life.
The chalky nothingness of gray
dull as your tarnished dreams.
Onset of another winter.

Late fall, 1910

Wedding

Your sister, pristine as a lily,
marries and moves to Brooklyn.
"We shall all miss Ethel," your mother writes Marcellus,
"I most of all, for she has been
my friend through all my tribulations,
always gentle and kind, never giving me
harsh words to grieve me."

But her leaving has cut you
as with the wind's sharp edge.
Who will now caution you against your brashness
without offending, guide you away from indiscretions
with quiet wisdom? Who will you whisper to
now under the eaves after the lanterns
are out and only the indifferent stars remain?

"Yes, Octavia misses her so much,"
your mother's note continues. "She took her leaving
so hard. Write to her often. Advise her
to go to Sunday school and church. Warn her
against her tongue and temper, her hasty
and unkind words. But don't let on
I mentioned anything to you."

November 27, 1910
202 South Drexel Street
Guthrie

26

Drexel Street

My dear Son,
Your long looked for letter came yesterday,
much to our joy and pleasure.
Of course I am not well but at work
and trying to keep up,
but sometimes I almost give out,
but I must try to keep on going
at least till someone else can take hold
and carry on.

I got this place in order that it might belong
to all of you children
and that all of you might pay for it
so that in the future
you might have a little piece of property
to live in or to be divided among yourselves.
I see no way now to get help,
only what Octavia can do.

I want Robert to come out there
as soon as he can, but I am not able
to send him now. I had big Drs. bills,
then I have a big bill from Ethel's wedding.
You know there was no one to give her a string
but Octavia and me.

I long to see the day I can rest.
I have worked and worked till now
I am just worked down and played out,
but how can I bear to see my children
have to take a back seat and come up short.

I hope we all may meet again with Ethel
in some near future day.
Write to her and Mr. Johnson.
He asked about you several times.

Your loving Mother.

202 South Drexel Street
Guthrie

Desert Song

Years in the desert have left me thirsty
and alone. No oasis calls me. My mouth is full
of the taste of sand. I am convinced I will die
of dehydrated dreams.

The pungent odor of rain teases my nostrils
with unkept promises. My tongue swells.
It is always high noon, and there is no tree
to cast a shadow. I have felt

the underground rumbling of trains
but where is the station where I may get on board?
I long to ride away from here before the talons
of vultures can tear apart this rotting flesh.

Octavia Long
December, 1910

IV.

Changes

Letters to Two Brothers

(Virginia Union University)

Dear Son,
Received yours of recent date announcing
your brother's arrival. Am glad to know
you both are doing well.

I had a card this morning from Octavia.
She had just been in Washington 12 hours
when she wrote it. I am expecting
a good long letter from her soon.

Take good care of Robert. It might be best
to let him have your job and you
find something else.
Let me hear from you.

Your affectionate father,
F.C. Long

Feby. 12, 1911
Hot Springs

Dear Rob,
Well, you two boys are together now.
You must make the most of opportunity.
Try to be satisfied. I am real glad
you and Sister decided to leave Guthrie.
It is such a dismal place.

I have had a short letter from Sister.
She likes Washington very much.
The school, she says, is a beautiful place.

Work hard, and write us when you can.
William wishes kindly to be remembered to you.

Your loving sister,
Ethel

February 23, 1911
Woodhaven, N.Y.

34

My dear Robbie,
I am better now and feeling pretty well.
The weather is very disagreeable,
the cause of so much sickness now.

How are you getting on? Do your best
to be contented. Remember things cannot be
always as we desire, but we can't lose time complaining.
You must have more courage. Strive toward a high
and honorable station in life. Do not be classed
with the slothful and mediocre. Work and depend
upon yourself.

I am sending $3.50 for you to buy some shoes.
Octavia said she is sending some money too.

Well, they are going to bring the capital
back to Guthrie, so they say. They are beginning
to look for a place to put the furniture.

You must practice your music all you can.
You will be glad some day for your piano training.

Love and kisses from your dear Mother

March 28, 1911
Guthrie

My dear Son,
How I do miss all you children.
How far are you from Octavia?
What is the fare to Washington?
Can't you go there some Friday evening
to see Octavia? Do so if you can.
She would feel better if she could see
some of you all.

Take care of Robbie. Make him keep on
plenty clothes. He better wear
his flannel underwear. Pneumonia
is so bad this time of year.

Your most devoted Mother,
Mrs. Sarah E. Long

P.S. Here is a piece of Ethel's wedding dress.
Keep it to look at.

May 28, '11
Guthrie

Mrs. Morris

Not like your sister's wedding, properly
announced, reported fondly in your mother's letters
detailing everything: a list of gifts, the guests, a piece of fabric
from her bridal gown,
the long train ride to Xenia, then on to Brooklyn.

From you, only a letter to your brother
in seminary in Virginia. "I have intended
for a week to write you. Not feeling very well,
I have procrastinated. Mr. Morris came up to New York
while I was there, and we were married Sunday, June 25th.
His father, in Philadelphia for the Baptist Alliance,
came over and performed the ceremony. Rev. Jernagin
from Oklahoma City came with Rev. Morris.
We had a very pleasant time.
Mama and Elias wish to be remembered to you."

Your wedding dress is lovely, the veil
a filmy coronet gracing your silken hair,
but your head tilts with a suggestion of defiance,
and your eyes are sharp as a dare.

July 6, 1911
202 N Street, N.W.
Washington, D.C.

Return

Whatever lure of freedom
that other world held out to you
turned false as thinly plated gold.
There is no hiding place
down here, and no escape.

Marriage mysteriously ended,
you return to Guthrie
and your maiden name.

The missing pages that could reveal
the truth are lost forever.

Late summer, 1912

Letter from Papa
(324 East Grant Street)

My dear Octavia,
I am pleased to find you
settled again in Guthrie
conveniently across the street
from the new high school
where you will teach.
It is most kind of Sergeant
and Mrs. Green to share their home
with you. Be assured that my hope
for your success and happiness
is constant as the sun.

It is only because I care
for you so much that I now caution you
about your careless speech.
Lately your usage has not been
commensurate with your training.
You are exposed to the criticism
of others who have less education.
If you are not careful, you will hear
of these complaints, and they will sound
unpleasant to you. I would advise
that you take up some good grammar text
and study it until
you have mastered the rules.

Another caution: Make it a point
to avoid involvement in the affairs
of others. Do not let your tongue speak
before your brain considers.
Failure to take this advice
will only cause you further grief.

I hope your mother is resting easy
and feeling better than when I left.
Look in on her
as often as you can.

Write to me at your convenience
and keep me informed of your progress.

Your affectionate father,
F.C. Long

September 10, 1912
Hot Springs

Reconciliation

What were you seeking? What did you find
that wasn't there before?
Had the times changed so much as to accept
your independent spirit,
or had you simply learned to juggle
the images of model teacher,
lady, and liberated woman before your time
without dropping any of the balls?

Weren't you more at peace then
with yourself and with the world around you
than you had ever been before?

Maybe you were disappointed
that life was not a challenge anymore,
only a cool and solid nugget
you could tuck inside your pocket
and secretly feel with your hand whenever
you needed reassurance.

Something you could take out and look at
late at night when you were alone
like a rare and costly jewel.

Maybe that was enough.

1912-1917
Guthrie

Toward Eternity

The live coals of your eyes
smolder like those of a tired mare
that has finished her journey.

Your hair's proud pompadour
is flat now as the Oklahoma plains.

Fashion has replaced your proper
high-collared dress of dark, ribboned brocade
with flimsy cotton, relaxed at the throat.

Often now you are too weary to meet
with after-school piano students.
Suddenly you are lonely,
your mother four years dead
and no one left in Guthrie
whose blood you share.
You worry the hours away
endlessly tatting towels
to make sleep come.

Mrs. Green is concerned about your cough,
your lack of energy. You open books of poetry
and read deep into the night.

In your broken sleep, you dream of horses
scaling the tops of houses. When
do you first suspect the direction
of their heads?

1918
324 East Grant Street
Guthrie

V.
Nightfall

Missouri

Robert's wife will not come near you.
Reluctantly she has agreed
to let you stay in the drafty barn,
but she begrudges you what meager comfort
such shelter can provide.

The isolation of a leper plagues you
like flies buzzing around an open wound.
You long for a tin cup of water
to cool the fever of long Missouri midnights.
You welcome the company of bats,
study with awe the symmetry of spiders' silk.

When the weak morning light finally
leaks through the planks, you drift
into deranged shadows of sleep.

Your brother stands by silent and sad.
Physician to others, he is helpless to cure
his own subordination to his wife's
indomitable will.

1919
St. Louis, Missouri

45

Rescue to Virginia

It was as if intoxicated demons
raged across the land
spewing their wrath into charged air
the day Marcellus came
and found you in such circumstances.

Only his pain was more intense,
for you had been his strength and inspiration,
his symbol of courage and improbable achievement,
and you had always felt for him a special bond
of tenderness and understanding.

Rescue you he must!
Without a map to guide him,
he began the only journey
love and duty would let him travel.

December 1919
St. Louis

Bedside Visit

"Marcellus, bring him to see me.
He need not come too close, but let me see
your firstborn child before I die."

Blood thicker than the red clay of Oklahoma,
stronger than the marriage bond
prevails. In spite of his wife's pleas
and protests, your brother dresses the boy
in clean bright rompers
and takes him to your bedside.

His wife, fearful for the child,
resentful of this test of loyalty,
screams in frustration, beats her fists
against the door. She thinks she may lose
the baby she is carrying.

It will be a week
before she speaks to him again
with tenderness.

January, 1920
Charlottesville, Virginia

At the River's Brink

"Come, Miss Octavia, let me plump your pillow
and prop you up awhile. You need to take
a little nourishment. Rev. Long will be here soon
and he will want to see his sister
with some color in her cheeks."

Even the slightest movement brings on
another spell of coughing. The neighbor
in whose home you are receiving care
hands you a clean rag. In a few minutes
she will fold the bloody sputum inside,
careful to touch only the dry edges,
and take it to the yard to burn.

Once quiet, you are too tired
to take the hot broth she has brought you.
All you want to do is sleep, and yet
you are afraid to close your eyes
for fear you will not open them again.

When he comes, he will stand near the door
fidgeting with his hat. How he will long
to hold you and kiss your fevered forehead,
but he has been cautioned. His wife and children
need him. He must not jeopardize
his health and theirs by touching you.

Both you and he will guard against
memories of shared childhood, thistles in the fields,
conspiratorial mischief. He will make
light talk, attempt a humorous remark or two.

Before he leaves, he will have a word of prayer,
risking his tentative emotions to invoke
God's intercession and His blessings on you.
Your death will be the keenest test of faith
that he will ever know.

February, 1920
Charlottesville

Message

The whimpers of his week-old son
rescued your brother from fractured sleep
Just as the message came. "Come!
She is fading fast. Come quickly!"

March 23, 1920
Charlottesville

VI.
Homing

Visit to Guthrie

Trunks full of brown letters,
brittle photographs,
and towels with tatted edges—
fragments of conversation heard in childhood—
a family Bible—notes hastily scribbled
in an old man's hand:

Because of these I came.

And that old piano that traveled
from Guthrie to Wilberforce
to New Rochelle to Detroit,
symbol of those whose fingers touched it,
whose voices rose above its dissonance
and made a melody:

Because of these I came.

May, 1987
Guthrie

708 South Second Street

A slim tree leans against this ruined house
forlorn and silent now, grieving
for long dead children.

The base is gutted by the curiosity of squirrels.
Gray siding falls away. Boards blind the windows
that once looked out on boys tossing a ball.

Around my face insects buzz coded messages
I cannot decipher. A kitten
peeps at me through the back fence.
Only a few short yards away
the rusty waters of Cottonwood Creek beckon.

Long ago the overflowing Cimarron River
reddened the gurgling creek. Disturbed now
only by a sluggish breeze, the waters murmur:
"Listen. Her footsteps often sounded
on the little bridge above me.
Her tears melted into my ripples.
If you are searching for her spirit, listen.
Be still and listen to my song."

May, 1987
Guthrie

Ladies of the Class of 1920

On sagging porches, in wheelchairs, in garden swings,
across unpaved streets from grazing cattle,
I find them—Miss Minnie Tilmon;
your friend Dorinda's sister, Beulah Wigley Smith;
Loletta Finley; Katherine Jackson Chadwick;
Vivian Hamilton—holding their own at 85.
"Octavia Long was my high school English teacher,"
they all tell me.

And one, ten years their senior,
puffing on a slim brown cigarette,
nails lacquered wicked red,
steady on high-heeled shoes:
"I knew the whole Long family.
Marcellus tried to court me
but I was too young for him."
And I: "Marcellus was my father."
"You must send me your picture."
I promise Ollie Matthews Fried I will.

Your photo in the Faver High School yearbook
of 1917. (Next year would be your last
before illness removed you to Missouri.)

"You look a lot like her. She was about
your size and color. You have her eyes."

I touch your ring of tiny pearls
that fits my finger still
and feel your hand closing over mine.

May, 1987
Guthrie

Greenwood Cemetery: Section MKG

I have come home to a land where
I have never been before

seeking to place missing puzzle
pieces in symmetry.

Grandfather whom I never knew,
can you feel my footsteps

over your grave? Do you approve
my proper grammar as

I whisper questions with no
answers among these weeds?

A sudden downpour anoints this
forgotten plot of earth.

The soil drinks deep awakening
your spirit. Is it your

voice the clouds bear? "Octavia, you've
come. At last you have come."

Hot Springs, Arkansas
May, 1984

At Rest

I searched for you and found you.
Now I leave a yellow rose
of remembrance on your grave.
Soon enough I will return
to join you in this sod, but
till then, I exorcize you
from my spirit, old skeleton
rattling around all these years
in my skin. Now be at peace.
Rest. Rest now. And so will I.

August 29, 1987
Mt. Olivet Cemetery
Richmond, Virginia

Epilogue

. . . . I heard somebody call my name
and I rose slowly through murky depths
of otherness until I reached the surface
and emerged at last into unfamiliar sunlight,
breathed the free air and swam
safely to shore.

The Long children (left to right):
Ethel, Robert, Octavia, and Marcellus

Naomi (left) and Octavia

". . . as a child I wore your face . . . ."

Ethel

" . . . always gentle and kind . . . ."

Octavia

Marcellus

Robert

Marcellus (standing) and Robert in later years

Sallie Long (right) with a first grade class at Lincoln School

Sarah (Sallie) and Frank Long

708 South Second Street in 1987
". . . forlorn and silent now . . . ."

202 South Drexel Street, then and now
" . . . a little piece of property . . . ."

Family History

Frank Cornelius Long, my paternal grandfather, was born in New Orleans, Louisiana, on March 2, 1857, the son of Alexander Dumas Long and Anna Mae Hawkins Long. This date is based on Leland University records bearing his own signature. A discrepancy in the year of birth, reported in 1915 in *Who's Who of the Colored Race* (edited by Frank Lincoln Mather) might be explained by his pending career relocation and his wish to be represented as a younger man than he was. He was of mixed heritage including African and French. He was known to have had one brother (or possibly half-brother), Robert Johnson, who had six children.

Frank was educated in the public schools of New Orleans after which he was converted to Christianity and baptized by the Rev. Henry Watts at the Springfield Baptist Church in Augusta, Georgia in January, 1875. It is suggested that at some point in his life he was employed by the federal government.

In October, 1876 Long enrolled at Leland University, located in New Orleans on the corner of St. Charles Avenue and Audubon Street near the present site of Tulane University. His curriculum included mathematics, history, science, philosophy, literature, composition and rhetoric, six courses in Greek, seven in Latin, and three in German. His transcript shows a grade point average close to 4.0. While at Leland he was apparently employed as a clerk at the Austerlitz Street Baptist Church which had close ties to the university. At Leland he met his future wife.

On May 24, 1881, the Ciceronian Literary Society of Leland University presented its annual exhibition program, consisting of recitations, speeches, songs, and a debate, at the Austerlitz Street church. Frank sang a tenor solo, "The Ivy Green," and Sarah Mumford, to whom he would be married the following month, made the farewell address. Shortly thereafter he earned his B.A. as Leland's first male graduate, with an M.A. coming later.

During the school year 1881-82, Frank taught mathematics at Bishop College in Marshall, Texas, where he was that institution's first full-time African American instructor. In the summer 1977 edition of *The Bishop Herald*, Dr. Melvin J. Banks wrote of him:

> . . . He insisted upon exactness in oral and written expression. He was a stickler for correctness in grammar and the best manners in stage decorum.
>
> Long and the President sponsored the Marston Literary and Debating Society which met every Friday evening . . . . The critic's report was scathing. Grammatical errors were pointed out. The manner in which the speakers presented themselves was a subject of rigid analysis. Many a country lad was inspired by this erudite Black teacher. Although he was with the College for only a year, leaving for graduate study at Chicago, Frank C. Long left a deep impression upon those who studied with him.

He took post-graduate courses at the University of Michigan and Kansas State Normal School and earned a Bachelor of Divinity degree at the Union Theological Seminary in Morgan Park, Illinois in 1884. He was graduated from the Stenographic Institute in Chicago in 1900.

A minister whose business card advertised him as a singing evangelist and "the man with a blackboard," he never seems to have pastored a church but earned his living as an educator.

Prior to 1900 the couple and their growing family did a considerable amount of moving throughout the Southwest, living in Independence, Missouri and Emporia, Kansas. In 1885, although they seldom had enough money, they purchased an oak piano which is now in my possession.

Records in the Oklahoma Territorial Museum in Guthrie indicate that "F.C. Long, colored" was principal of Lincoln School there in 1900, but his name does not appear in any subsequent city records. In 1901 or shortly thereafter, he evidently left the dismal little town without his family in his perpetual quest for more challenging employment. While Frank kept in close touch with his children and was involved in their lives, he never lived with his family again.

Settling in Hot Springs, Arkansas, he became principal of the Rugg Street School which, after a fire, was rebuilt as Langston High School, producing its first graduating class in 1910. He took great pride in the curriculum offered, describing Langston as "a first-class colored high school" which offered four years each of Latin, English, science, history, and mathematics. Its graduates, he boasted, "have easily found entrance into freshmen classes of leading American colleges."

His position in Hot Springs was the most permanent one in his career. By 1915, he was ready to make a change. Letters of recommendation from such persons as the mayor of Hot Springs, a member of the board of education, and the superintendent of the State Department of Education gave him superior recommendations for his character, vigor, educational qualifications, leadership, and community involvement. In spite of these letters of support, he evidently failed to secure the position he sought as head of the normal school in Pine Bluff and subsequently moved to Memphis, Tennessee, where he taught and occasionally preached.

Before leaving Hot Springs, his wife having died in 1914, he married Sarah Baker, who worked as an attendant at one of the white bath houses. She remained in Hot Springs when he moved to Memphis.

In 1924 Long suffered the first of a series of paralyzing strokes. His wife took him back to Hot Springs where she cared for him faithfully, first at 215 Silver Street, and then, under severe financial strain, at 6 Helem Street, a house owned by her family. He died November 15, 1928 and was buried in a section of Greenwood Cemetery originally owned by Union Baptist Church, where he was a member, and another Black church.

In 1994 I located his grave and replaced the broken chunk of marble that served as a headstone with a more appropriate marker. His second wife, who died in 1967, lies beside him.

According to Leland University records, **Sallie E.K. Mumphord,** my grandmother, was born on April 27, 1860 in DeWitt County, Texas, and was baptized in Victoria, Texas by the Rev. Mitchell Harrison in 1871. Her mother was or had been a slave and her father was a native American of the Cherokee tribe. Full-blooded or not, he and his children qualified for government land in Hugoton, Kansas. I do not know if the couple were married, but there was evidently a son William also born of this union. The mother later married or remarried and gave birth to at least two more children, James and DeLois Arthur.

Sallie entered Leland University in December, 1878 and during her college years her name appears in a street directory in another part of Texas with the same spelling. However, she is listed as Sarah Mumford on the program of the university's Ciceronian Society in 1881, a month before her marriage to Frank. She evidently left Leland without graduating, completing her education at the normal school in Emporia, Kansas.

It is my guess that, when Frank decided to leave Guthrie, Oklahoma after only one year there as a principal, Sarah was simply tired of moving and decided to remain in the place where she could find some stability. Guthrie became the most permanent of the family's various abodes.

Left alone with her four children in 1901 or 1902, she lived at 708 South Second Street and taught first grade at Lincoln School. Copies of her teaching certificates bearing test scores show that she was well qualified although there are occasional grammatical lapses in her letters. This tiny rented house was located between Cottonwood Creek, which occasionally flooded, and the railroad tracks. Suffering from poor health, she found the struggle for survival difficult. As there was no high school in Guthrie which African Americans could attend, she had to provide for her children's education elsewhere. To what extent her absent husband contributed to these expenses I do not know.

Seeking more security, she sold her farm in Hugoton in 1910 and made a down payment on a house at 202 South Drexel Street. With the children starting new phases of their lives and her health failing, she eventually moved to 1002 East Springer Street, possibly renting out the house.

A woman of strong determination and courage, excellent character, and high ideals, she was the strength of the family through all kinds of hardship and adversity and was deeply devoted to her children. Her middle-class values were not false but were a reflection of the period and culture with which she was familiar.

Sallie E.K. Mumphord (or Sarah Mumford Long) died in Guthrie on April 21, 1914 and was buried beside her mother in Victoria, Texas, a small wooden cross marking her grave.

Octavia Cornelia Long, the eldest of the Long children, was born in Waco, Texas on June 14, 1885. My brother seemed to recall hearing our father say that oil was discovered on Octavia's government-granted land in Hugoton and it was sold. If this is true, it would account for her having the funds to attend high school in Lawrence, Kansas, graduating in the class of 1904. Her class card lists Hot Springs as her home address, suggesting that her father assumed some financial responsibility for her education. She remained in Lawrence, earning a Bachelor of Arts degree in English in 1909. Under her picture in the 1909 issue of *The Jayhawker* are written the words: "A hard working student, always striving for the best grade in her class."

At various times she took classes at Bishop College, but for the next two years she taught fifth grade at Douglas

School, one of the two elementary schools for Black students in Guthrie.

Guthrie was often described in negative terms, and Octavia found it even more dismal after her sister married and moved away. She had been corresponding with Elias A. Morris, whose family were friends of the Longs, and in January or early February of 1911, she moved to Washington, DC. where he lived. She found employment there as a teacher.

On a Sunday in June of that year, on a visit to New York to visit her sister, and with her mother present, Elias and Octavia were married in a small ceremony. The officiating minister was the bridegroom's father, the Rev. Elias C. Morris, a prominent Baptist minister, who had gone east to attend a convention. The newlyweds lived at 200 N Street, N.W. in Washington, D.C.

But the marriage was short-lived. I do not know if there was a divorce, but Octavia returned to Guthrie in 1912, using her maiden name, in time to teach English at the newly-constructed Faver High School, the first high school for African Americans in that city. She lived across the street from the school at 324 East Grant Street in the home of "Sergeant" Green and his family, friends of the Longs. (Her mother, in failing health, was then at the Springer Street address.)

Although she dated a Bill Martin, Octavia never remarried. She continued to teach, her photograph in the 1917 yearbook, until tuberculosis cut short her career. With no family members left in Guthrie, she went to live with her brother Robert, then a physician, whose wife Shirley resented the Long family because of their light skin color. Probably also afraid of contagion, she placed Octavia in a barn-like structure behind the house. When her other brother discovered her circumstances, he removed her to Charlottesville, Virginia, where he was living. She died on March 23, 1920 and was laid to rest in the family plot newly purchased by her brother in Mt. Olivet Cemetery in Richmond, Virginia,, my mother's birthplace.

Ethel Elizabeth Long was born in Waco, Texas on June 4, 1887. She was graduated from Topeka (Kansas) Training and Normal School, where she met William E. Johnson, an instructor in business and commerce. She taught one of the early elementary grades at Lincoln School where her mother also taught. Along with her father she attended "the Chicago University" for twelve weeks in the summer of 1910, studying music and other subjects.

On November 9, 1910, she and Mr. Johnson were married at the family's newly acquired home on Drexel Street. Octavia played the piano and sang at the wedding, which seems to have observed all the rules of propriety although I do not know if her father was present. The couple visited the bridegroom's mother in Xenia, Ohio, where additional gifts and a reception awaited them. Then they took the train to New York where, at William's suggestion, they "passed" in order to avoid the inconvenience of Jim Crow facilities.

The Johnsons settled at 1019 Union Avenue, Ozone Park, Brooklyn (later listed as Woodhaven), New York. William entered government service at the navy yard. Three sons were born of this union, Harold Eugene, Kenneth Lowell, and William, Jr.

The family later moved to the campus of Wilberforce University in Ohio where William held the position of custodian of buildings and grounds for more than forty years.

Ethel eventually went blind from inoperable glaucoma but adjusted well to this inconvenience, still able to perform her household chores. She died in Xenia, Ohio on July 13, 1965 and is buried there. Her descendants include three sons, five grandchildren, and five great-grandchildren.

Clarence Marcellus Long, my father, was born in Victoria, Texas on August 25, 1888 in the tiny home of his maternal grandmother. He was baptized in 1897 in Emporia, Kansas by the Rev. S.S. Jones who remained his mentor and spiritual father for life. (In 1899 Rev. Jones founded the First

Baptist Church in Guthrie where the Long family were members.) Called Marcellus by his family and friends, he completed college preparatory and printing courses in the academy at Bishop College and taught printing there while still a student. Notebooks containing some of his "orations" written at Bishop reveal a keen intellect and an excellent foundation in composition, history, and classical literature. Oklahoma Territorial Museum records indicate that he worked as a printer for *The Oklahoma Safeguard,* a Black weekly newspaper, from 1908 to 1910.

A letter from a friend during his Bishop years refers to his decision to enter the ministry. He was licensed to preach in Langston on May 20, 1909. In spite of his father's initial discouragement, "Son" walked the two or three blocks to the little railroad station in Guthrie, carrying a cardboard suitcase and wearing a summer suit, the only one he owned, in January or February, 1910, arriving in Richmond, Virginia with 25 dollars to his name. He petitioned the president for any kind of labor in exchange for his expenses and was permitted to work his way through a three-year course in theology in two and a half years, sometimes earning income by preaching at various churches, including one in Waverly. He also worked as a waiter in Cape May, New Jersey during the summers. (When his brother arrived the following year, equally destitute, he persuaded the president to let him too enroll and work his way through the university.)

Now an ordained minister holding a Bachelor of Theology degree, he began a 63-year career as a clergyman as pastor of Third Baptist Church in Hampton. He married Maude Selena Hilton, my mother, a native of Richmond, on September 3, 1913. The following year he became pastor of First Baptist Church in Charlottesville (1914-1921), where my brothers were born, followed by Bank Street Baptist Church (1921-1925), where I was born.

While pastor of Calvary Baptist Church in East Orange, New Jersey (1925-1937), he earned his Bachelor of Arts degree at Upsala College, where he was valedictorian of his class, and his Master of Arts in church history at Drew University in Madison. Virginia Union University conferred on him the Doctor of Divinity degree on June 5, 1929. During the Depression he taught classes part time in Negro literature and sociology in the federally-funded (Works Progress Administration) adult education program. His travels included a summer-long visit in 1934 to the World Baptist Alliance in Berlin, other parts of Europe, Egypt, and the Holy Land.

Marcellus was pastor of the historic Central Baptist Church in St. Louis, Missouri from 1937 to 1942 and of Bethesda Baptist Church in New Rochelle, New York from 1942 until his retirement in 1968. He was responsible for the restoration of the building following a fire and the addition of an attached educational center. He was the first African American to be appointed to a Board of Education in the state of New York, serving in New Rochelle for ten years.

Following his retirement he and my mother moved to Detroit, Michigan to be near me. He continued to be in demand as a guest preacher into his 86th year. He died in Detroit on April 1, 1976 of viral pneumonia. He is buried near his sister Octavia in Mt. Olivet Cemetery in Richmond, Virginia, where my mother now also rests. The standing marker in the cemetery bears the name Long on one side and Hilton on the other. On the Hilton side lie my maternal grandparents, an aunt and an uncle. Marcellus' descendants include two sons and a daughter, six grandchildren, and four great-grandchildren.

There is some discrepancy in the reported birthplace of **Robert Elliott Long,** but according to my father's records, he was born in Fort Smith, Arkansas on July 15, 1892. He attended Faver High School in 1909 which, I assume, met in a church or private home since the school building had not yet been erected. As a boy he worked for awhile for the *Guthrie Daily Leader,* earning five dollars a week. Undecided about his career goals, he joined his brother at Virginia Union University at the beginning of 1911, evidently with some financial assistance from his father. He was later graduated from Meharry Medical College in Nashville, Tennessee.

He and his wife Shirley lived in Oklahoma somewhere near Gurthrie for awhile, later relocating in St. Louis, Missouri where he spent the rest of his life, except for about four years spent in Hannibal. He had his own medical practice and served at various times on the staffs of the old St. Mary's Infirmary, People's Hospital, and Homer Phillips Hospital. He continued to volunteer in the clinic at Homer Phillips for three years after his retirement and to practice at his home at 4619 McMillan Avenue until he was 82 years old.

In 1958 he self-published a book of his verse, *Levity, Legend, and Sentiment,* which includes two poems of autobiographical significance, one referring to the good times spent during childhood trips to Galveston, Texas, and the other concerning the oak piano and the family singing around it as he sat on his mother's knee.

Widowed in 1974, Robert eventually lost his sight to glaucoma and spent his last years in a nursing home, cared for by friends. He died on January 17, 1982, the last of his generation (as I am now the last of mine) and is buried in St. Peter's Cemetery in St. Louis. He had no children.

Descendants of Frank Cornelius Long (1857-1928) and Sallie E.K. Mumphord Long (1860-1914)

Octavia Cornelia Long (1885-1920)

Ethel Elizabeth Long (1887-1965) *(with William E. Johnson)*

    Harold Eugene Johnson (1912-1981) *(with Camille Cotter Taylor)*
        Sylvia Penelope Johnson (1947-) *(with Robert Aulston)*
            Alexander McKenzie Aulston (1973-)
            Damon Taylor Aulston (1977-)
            Nicholas Jay Aulston (1980-)
        Harold Eugene Johnson, Jr. (1951-) *(with Cathrine Berry)*
        James Morris Johnson (1987-)

    Kenneth Lowell Johnson (1915-1984) *(with Evelyn Belle Lewis)*
        Kenneth Lowell Johnson, Jr. (1944-)*(with Mary Dell Parker)*
            Kenneth Lowell Johnson, III (1971-)
        Marilyn Elaine Johnson (1949-1978)

    William E. Johnson, Jr. (c. 1920-1972) *(wife unknown)*
        William E. Johnson, III (c. 1950)

Clarence Marcellus Long (1888-1976) *(with Maude Selena Hilton)*

    Clarence Marcellus Long, Jr., (1918-1978)*(with Laverne Stansberry)*
        Cheryl Marie Long (1949-)
        Patricia Ann Long (1950-) *(with Michael Wyatt Tucker)*
            Michael Wyatt Tucker, II (1976-)
        Clarence Marcellus Long, III (1954-)

    Wilbur Franklin Long (1920-1998) *(with Katie Marie Butler)*
        Kathy Etolia Long (1956-1997) *(with Severo Antonio Bonilla)*
            Victoria Marie Bonilla (1990-)
            Alexandra Antonia Bonilla (1992-)
        Karen Octavia Long (1958-) *(with Peter C. Rowe)*
            Cody Quentin Rowe (1996-)

    Naomi Cornelia Long (1923-) (with Julian Fields Witherspoon)
        Jill Annette Witherspoon (1947-) *with Edward J. Boyer)*
            Liliana Malaika Boyer (1975-)

Robert Elliott Long (1892-1982)